HEARTWORK
OF THE SOUL
YOUR TRAINING GUIDE TO EMOTIONAL WELLNESS

JOANNA AVIN

HeartWork® of The Soul
Your Training Guide To Emotional Wellness
Joanna Avin

Copyright © March 2024 by Joanna Avin

All rights reserved. No part of this publication may be reproduced, distributed, or transmitted in any form or by any means, including photocopying, recording, or other electronic or mechanical methods, without the prior written permission of the publisher, except in the case of brief quotations embodied in critical reviews and certain other noncommercial uses permitted by copyright law.

For permission requests, write to the publisher, addressed "Attention: Permissions Coordinator," at adminservices@pecantreebooks.com

For author speaking or workshops requests,
please visit www.heartworkprecision.com

ISBN: 979-8-9884334-4-6 (Paperback)
ISBN: 979-8-9884334-5-3 (Digital)
Library of Congress Control Number: 2024907444
Front Cover Artwork and Design by Doran Francis
Interior Design by Marigold Emal
Diagrams Designed by Cassia Garrett

Pecan Tree Publishing
Hollywood, FL 33020
www.pecantreebooks.com

New Voices, New Styles, New Vision
Empowering Authors with Impactful Stories
www.pecantreebooks.com
@pecantreepub – on all social media
Hollywood, FL

ABOUT THE AUTHOR

Joanna Avin is the founding President/CEO of HeartWork® Precision (www.heartworkprecision.com), a training and development company dedicated to strengthening the souls of individuals to become emotionally intelligent leaders. For over 15 years, she has partnered with corporations, non-profit organizations, and clients seeking transformational growth.

Certified by High Performing Systems, Joanna is a seasoned Emotional Intelligence Coach, and a sought-after speaker. She encourages her clients to lean into their discomfort to become the difference they want to see personally and professionally. As a result of her passion and drive, countless lives have been changed. Leaders are excelling, broken families are being restored, clients are evolving from the mindset of being a victim to becoming victorious, and the work continues.

Maya Angelou said, "I've learned that people will forget what you said, people will forget what you did, but people will never forget how you made them feel." These words drive Joanna to make a difference: one person, one organization, and one audience at a time.

PEOPLE ARE TALKING ABOUT HEARTWORK® OF THE SOUL

HeartWork® of The Soul helps identify ~~the~~ emotions that drive our decisions. A better understanding of these emotions leads to more favorable outcomes when making those decisions. Joanna takes the painstaking opportunity to put these pillars to the test. I have witnessed the transformative journey that emotional intelligence provided her. This book will take you through a great journey of self-discovery and self-healing. The pillars discussed will lay the groundwork for emotional growth and breakthrough. It has helped me to become a better husband, father, friend, and entrepreneur.

Michael P. Avin

In today's world, human connection and community are more important than ever, but they can also be difficult to achieve. *HeartWork® of The Soul* is a book that helps readers explore and understand their emotions in a way that promotes self-awareness and personal growth while also fostering healthy relationships with others. Our emotions are a powerful force that can't be ignored, but with the right tools, we can learn to manage them to protect ourselves and others, even in conflict. This book is a guide to help you understand the root of your emotions and develop the emotional intelligence needed to create strong, healthy relationships.

This book is perfect for helping you take the first step towards a better and more stable life.

Kevin M. Tucker, *KMT Enterprises*
Author, Speaker, and Leadership & Relationship Strategist

Amazing Results From HeartWork® Course Participants

The Emotional Intelligence strategies you provided allowed me to learn more about myself and improve how I "show up." I recommend this book to everyone, not just those in leadership. The more people in workplace environments understand the value of emotional intelligence, the better our communication, customer service, and culture will be.

Kelly M.

A few days before the emotional intelligence class you facilitated, I was in the worst place of my life, not realizing that I was there because I was stubborn, and I overestimated myself in things I knew little about. During your class you really showed me a lot. It's like you took my soul out of my body to show how I reflect everyone around me. The experience was amazing. You saved me from myself, because I was not able to realize how the energy I put out affected people, which led me to a dark and lonely place in my life. I'm very thankful you gave me a layout to guide me through life with a different perspective so that I continue to grow and evolve.

Jerry G.

Ms. Avin, your emotional intelligence course was timely, enlightening and extremely helpful (for too many reasons to list here). You are the perfect person for teaching this self-awareness and self-management course. Your energy and interactive style is one of the best I have had the pleasure of learning from. This course will positively affect my relationships both personally and professionally. I wish to take this course again to unpack even more than the first time.

Donald S.

CONTENTS

FOREWORD – Pastor Henry B. Fernandez,
          The Faith Center 13
INTRODUCTION 15
How to Read this Book 21
PART I—Are You Feeling Some Type of Way? 25
PART II—Are You Babysitting Spinach? 36
PART III—Get It Togetha...54
PART IV—Sick and Tired of Being Sick and Tired? 68
PART V—Are You Really Sorry to Hear That? 81
Acknowledgments 95
Appendix...99
Citations 101

FOREWORD

I have known Joanna for many years. She has shown a heart for serving others and the skill to reach them. As her pastor, I have seen her grow in the faith and embrace her gifts.

This book is the culmination of years of study, practical experience, and divine inspiration. Joanna has immersed herself in the study of emotional intelligence because she understands that growth starts when we begin to understand ourselves. She has trained thousands of people to unleash their potential by digging deep into themselves and doing the hard work of HeartWork®.

From self-awareness to forgiveness and understanding emotions you may have repressed or suppressed, this book is designed to help you become the person God has created you to be. As a spiritual leader, I have felt compelled to help God's people maximize their potential because when we understand purpose and how it relates to the work God has placed each of us here to accomplish, then we bring glory to God and collectively help the world become a better place. I hope this book blesses you and becomes a valuable tool on your journey to become better, stronger, and more impactful.

Now, let's begin doing the HeartWork®.

Henry B. Fernandez, Senior Pastor
The Faith Center
Sunrise, FL

INTRODUCTION

"What goes on in the house stays in the house!" "Kids are to be seen and not heard." "Fix your face, or I'll give you something to cry about." "Be strong." These are some of the statements that many of us heard growing up, especially those raised in ethnic communities. The words could be heard in homes, schools, churches, etc., from adult to child. Many parents were simply using verbiage their parents, aunts, uncles, or other family members used with them. The cycle of suppressing and crippling emotions begins with negative family communication. Generations later, those children become the parents who continue toxic patterns. Where will this cycle end? Who is going to ensure that their family won't have to deal with the same unhealthy emotional patterns as the previous generations? This change will begin with you. My goal is to help you begin to learn some new emotional practices that will forever change the way you interact with your family and others.

Emotions have been given a negative connotation for centuries. I will focus on and introduce emotions in a way that may be unfamiliar, but I believe enlightening. When we first entered the world, we could not accept or reject our guardians' perspectives. We became a product of our upbringing, culture, trauma, and societal conditioning. You were fed ideologies on handling emotions – based on your gender - that forced you to adapt accordingly. As you grew, you were nuanced into the culture of your home and environment. This is where the separation began. Hence, boys' and girls' emotional experiences are shaped differently.

Are women more emotional than men? What do you think? I have posed this question in every emotional intelligence class that I have facilitated. According to a University of Michigan study[1], little to no emotional differences were found between men and women. The study suggests that men's emotions fluctuate to the same extent as women's, although likely for different reasons. The question of which sex is more emotional sets the stage for the discussion of the origin of cultural or societal conditioning in handling emotions. Many boys were taught that emotions were for girls and not them. Boys weren't supposed to cry or express how they were feeling. Many boys were taught that they needed to be the protector and provider. If boys expressed emotions, they may have been considered weak and become prey to bullies.

On the contrary, many girls were allowed to express their emotional selves and encouraged to confront friends with whom they had conflicts. As a result, many women seem to be more emotionally expressive. However, males and females were both born with six primitive emotions (unless there was some type of developmental disorder). These emotions are happiness, sadness, anger, fear, surprise, and disgust[2]. These emotions arise spontaneously without provocation. If you think about these emotions in their beginning stages, they don't require your decision to bubble to the surface. You don't have to teach a baby to feel any of these emotions; they are triggered based on outside stimuli. As we develop, these emotions become nuanced by society, culture, upbringing, etc., and as a result, we have learned to suppress or express emotions when they arise. Emotions play such a pivotal role in our decision-making that we must understand the art of finding balance when we are in a heightened emotional state of mind.

We must also learn how to properly navigate emotions to have a healthy sense of self as well as healthy relationships with others. Success in this area requires emotional intelligence. So, what is emotional intelligence?

Emotional Intelligence Versus Intelligence Quotient

Emotional Intelligence (or EI) is the ability to understand and manage your own emotions, as well as recognize and influence the emotions of those around you[3]. Emotional Quotient (EQ) reflects the level of a person's emotional intelligence, often as represented by a score in a standardized test. Although these concepts are similar it is important to understand the difference between the two. For example, although many people have been taught the basics of swimming there are levels to swimming experience. Early in the training one may be considered a survivor, a beginner swimmer. As they continue to train, they may ultimately become an international elite swimmer. What makes the difference? The training consistently pursued. Likewise, when it comes to being emotionally intelligent, there are levels of competence that drive one's success. Unfortunately, many don't understand the difference between emotional intelligence and intelligence quotient. No matter how smart you are, your success may be determined by another variable.

Intelligence Quotient (IQ) is an assessment of one's ability to think and reason. In earlier years, the IQ test was a determining factor in one's success. Researchers surmise that if Theoretical Physicist Albert Einstein took an IQ test, he would be considered a genius. Based on the findings from specific types of people who took these tests and their interests, society began to push the need for IQ in potentially determining long-term wealth. However, many psychologists began to question the validity of IQ scores, citing research and discovery into additional areas of the mind that also contributed to success. Psychologist Daniel Goleman continued the work of Psychologists John Mayer and Peter Salovey, popularizing the term emotional intelligence in the 1990's. Through his work and other pioneers of emotional intelligence, they determined that EI was the key factor in one's personal and professional success. When we look at the truly extraordinary people who inspire countless people and make a difference in varying spheres, you see they do this by connecting with people on a personal and emotional level. What differentiates them is not their IQ but their EI – their emotional intelligence. Many of us were taught that getting a degree or some type of certification was an indicator of success in life. However, several studies have proven that one's EQ is a better contributor to success in life. Several studies revealed the following EQ statistics: 90 percent of top performers have high EQ, EQ is responsible for 58 percent of your job performance, and people with high EQ make $29,000 more annually than their low EQ counterparts[4]. These stats indicate the power of being emotionally intelligent. We have all met individuals who have several letters – noting their degrees achieved - behind their name, plenty of money in the bank, power, or fame; yet they still lead miserable lives. Many celebrities have ended their lives because material things could not satisfy the emotional needs that were calling from within. Change begins on the inside. Attempting to address the outside without understanding the inside is like putting lipstick on a pig. No matter how intentional you are about dressing the pig differently, it is still a pig. Internal work is needed to address external decisions and the work required to do so is not instinctive. This type of work requires a particular skill set, intentionality, and HeartWork®.

HeartWork®

What is HeartWork®? HeartWork® is the process of managing dormant or flared emotions to start the healing and restoration of one's soul. According to Timothy Jorgensen, minister, and author of *Spirit Life Training*, we are three-part beings[5]. Humans are spiritual beings who possess a soul and live in a body. We will focus our attention on the soul which is made up of five basic areas: emotion, intellect/reasoning, memory, imagination, and will[6]. Imagine the soul as the house, and the rooms of the house are the five basic areas. This reading will zone in on the room called emotions and requires HeartWork®.

I realized in facilitating classes that this type of work is pivotal in emotional wellness. When participants embraced the HeartWork® challenges, they felt a suppressed emotional weight lifted. How do I know? I've learned that the best teachers are those who have experienced and overcome what they are teaching. That was my story. Every challenge I present, I execute in my own life. HeartWork® is not something that you will ever master. It is something that will continually teach you. As I began doing the work, I became aware of the emotional baggage gripping my soul and driving unhealthy decisions. So, I had to do the HeartWork® of my soul and discover, manage, and forgive at times when I didn't have the drive to do so. This work taught me critical lessons that left me with confidence, understanding my values, and navigating healthier relationships with others. This process doesn't feel good, and it may seem, at times, that everything, internally and externally, is trying to delay or stop the work. But persist. The work is good for you! It's like going to the gym and feeling sore a day or two later. If you allow that soreness to stop you from going back to the gym, you will never achieve the results you desire. There must be continual effort to be better and we are responsible for how we are showing up in life.

Many times, we blame others for how they treat us, what they do to us, or what they say to us. However, *you teach people how to treat you* and *if you don't stand up for yourself, you deserve what you accept*. We are where we are because of the decisions that we made or didn't make. We must begin to release some of the weight that has been wearing us down year after year and stop making excuses or looking for reasons to justify our poor behavior. Future generations depend on our ability to get things right. Are you up for the HeartWork® challenge?

HOW TO READ THIS BOOK

To begin the journey of heart change, imagine that you are building your house. You must have a blueprint that lays out the specifications and shows what the finished product should look like. You will also need the essential materials (concrete and wood) for a firm foundation. As you read, you will be provided the blueprint, concrete, and wood to maximize your understanding of EI thus building your home. First, we must begin to set your blueprint. What are some areas within that you are looking to improve upon?

_____

_____

Now that you have identified those areas, which attributes are you looking to embrace and walk in? These answers help to determine your blueprint of success.

_____

_____

I'm glad that you have set the stage for your growth and development. Let's continue your home-building process. When one begins to build a house, the framework of the home is outlined. The framework in our process is understanding emotions and how they impact our decisions, body, and future. After the framework has been outlined, cinder blocks are required to begin setting the structure of a house. The cinderblocks are represented by four major pillars of EI, according to Daniel Goleman. These areas are Self-Awareness, Self-Regulation, Motivation, and Empathy. These pillars require great attention to detail for the overall support and the stability of your house.

SELF-AWARENESS

Self-awareness is the ability to recognize and understand our moods, emotions, and drivers, as well as their effects on ourselves and others. *Awareness is the seed of personal growth and development.* Many people boast about their level of awareness, not realizing what is at the root of their behaviors and decision-making. Although you may have knowledge of an issue within, it doesn't mean you are truly aware. Awareness comes in stages and ultimately evokes a change or hard reset in one's attitude. If your level of awareness is not changing your attitude concerning a thing, then you haven't reached the seed. For example, many people know that they need to lose weight and know what it will take to lose weight, but they aren't able to actually lose it. Once you have discovered the seed of your inability to lose weight, then you can begin to manage yourself differently. In Part II, Are You Babysitting Spinach, you will learn that you don't know what you don't know but there is hope. Hope begins when you decide to reset your attitude, change directions, and begin the regulation process.

SELF-REGULATION

Self-Regulation, the second pillar of EI for your home, is the ability to manage disruptive emotions and impulses, and to think before you react. Many people don't manage their emotions; instead, they attempt to control them in the moment. This is-extremely dangerous. In the heat of a moment emotions are in a heightened state, and there is a greater chance that things will be communicated, and behaviors demonstrated that you may regret once emotions subside. This type of work takes a level of motivation and discipline to achieve true mastery. It absolutely captures the old saying, "if you stay ready you never have to get ready." Self-Regulation places you in the driver seat of your emotions and discipline creates the consistency needed for overall success.

MOTIVATION & DISCIPLINE

The third pillar of EI for your home includes motivation and discipline. Motivation is defined as a general willingness or desire of someone to do something. Discipline is the practice of training people to obey rules or a code of behavior. Both are needed in accomplishing and achieving better actions and behaviors. Unfortunately, even with our best attempts and intentions we will fall short, and empathy will be needed.

EMPATHY

The fourth pillar that we will discuss in EI for your home is empathy. Empathy is the ability to understand and relate with the emotions of others or yourself. At times we can be our own worst critic. We can easily see the good in and for others, but unfortunately, it's difficult to see the good within ourselves when we fall short This pillar will focus on the areas needed to sustain a positive state of mind on your journey. You will always fall but what will it take for you to get back up and push on? How do you show empathy to others as you navigate this path? This chapter will give you practical tools to assist you in your heart change.

The four pillars of EI, Self-Awareness, Self-Regulation, Motivation, and Empathy set the framework of your house and helps you achieve the look that you desire. Through each portion of this book, you will gain the materials needed to build, support, and beautify your home. You are the General Contractor of your home. No one should research what is needed to build a home, gather the materials, begin the building process, and decide to quit in the beginning stages. I encourage you to reflect, meditate, and complete the HeartWork® Challenges; use this book as the blueprint for your emotional home. It will ensure all the materials are utilized properly, installed successfully, so you can have the finished product of your aspirations. Ready, set, build!

PART I

Are You Feeling Some Type of Way?

Have you ever been in a situation where you said something or behaved in a way that embarrassed you after things settled? You wish you would've stopped yourself prior to unleashing toxic statements. The more unfortunate part is that you released that venom on your child, spouse, family member, co-worker, etc. Now you must continue in relationship with them, but shame and guilt has settled in your heart. It has become hard for you to continue to look them in the eye or be around them without feeling a level of embarrassment. The good news is there are strategies to avoid the feelings that come after a corrupt conversation or toxic behavior. You can avoid feeling some type of way by learning the tools that will put you on the offense rather than performing damage control.

Let's begin by defining emotions. Emotions are energy in your feelings that can drive you to or away from action. According to Psychology Today, emotions drive 80 percent of the choices Americans make, while practicality and objectivity only represent about 20 percent of decision-making[7]. Research by Dr. Travis Bradberry indicates that only 34 percent of the time are we able to recognize and identify what we are feeling in the moment[8]. This indicates that an estimated 46 percent of the time we are making decisions based on how we feel in the moment. Think about this, almost 50 percent of your decisions are based on your brain operating on autopilot. Have you driven to a location and when you arrived you don't remember driving there? It's almost as if the car drove itself, pretty scary. Now think about that autopilot state of mind response as it relates to your finances, choosing who you will be in a relationship with, having children or not, your career path, etc. Since we can operate on autopilot 50 percent of the time, emotional intelligence is absolutely needed. Emotional Intelligence is a skill set that requires conscious thinking and patience.

Diagram A1

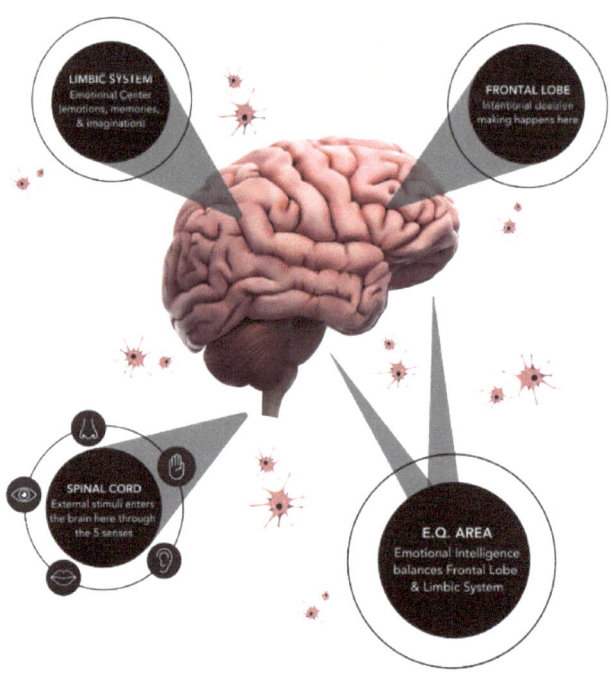

LIMBIC SYSTEM

Our brain is built to default on emotions initially. Diagram A1 shows a basic illustration of the way our brain is set up. When we are presented with external situations our brain begins to gather data. Information is sent through our five senses, what we see, hear, touch, smell, and taste. This data enters our brain through our spinal cord and enters our limbic system. The Limbic System is the area of the brain that has multiple functions[9]. One of the functions in the limbic system is to allow us to feel emotions when faced with external data. This is also the area where our amygdala is located which stores our memories. So, your memories and emotions are stored in the same area of the brain. This is why when you think about a memory you immediately begin to feel the emotions that you were experiencing at that time. This is good to have but can also be dangerous to your reality.

Many of us are making decisions as adults based on unresolved emotions as a child. For example, imagine a seven-year-old girl is happily riding her bike down the sidewalk. Suddenly, a dog comes out of nowhere, jumps on her, and begins to attack her. All through life she never talks about her incident with the dog but chooses not to own pets. Now, which emotions do you think she experienced as a little girl? Maybe fear, surprise, anxiousness, etc. Now this little girl is 35 years old and jogging in the park. As she settles into her run, suddenly, a dog comes out of nowhere. What emotions do you think she experiences at that time? The same emotions she felt at seven years old. Unfortunately, because she never addressed the original incident, she has hibernated fear. Consequently, if she never receives therapy or healing, a trauma imprint can be left in her soul that will impact her reality and possibly her future generations. Many of us have experienced situations or events that have left emotional scars in our heart. Can you identify a memory that occurred earlier in life that you have built into your decision making as an adult? Did you get therapy or speak through that incident with someone? Have you allowed that memory to dictate your future generations? It's time to do something different. Your soul needs restoration. Let's take a look at another area of the brain that is responsible for our rational thoughts.

FRONTAL LOBE

The front of your brain is called the frontal lobe.[10] This area is your risk and reward center. This area allows you to weigh the long- and short-term consequences of a decision. Almost 50 percent of our decision making never makes it to this area. Which suggests that many of our decisions are emotionally hijacked by the limbic system.

Research determined that one of the main differences between our brain and the brain of an animal is the frontal lobe[11]. Animals operate solely from their natural instincts. They don't have the capacity to think about the short- or-long-term consequences of their actions. Think about a dog that is loose on the street that may be angry or scared and begins to terrorize the neighborhood. He begins to attack people trying to subdue him. What happens? Authorities may get called, the dog will be restrained and kept in a cage, maybe a muzzle is placed on him, possibly euphemism is decided as his fate. All because he acted irrationally and became a danger to the community. Now, I want you to imagine a human being that is enraged. People try to assist him before he becomes a danger to himself or other people. What structures are put in place to control a human that is behaving irrationally? When we don't take the time to engage our frontal lobe (when our emotions are intense) and make intentional decisions from that place, we become a liability. Sometimes, authorities have to engage the situation. That is not something that any of us should want. Before that happens, remember that it's your choice to engage your frontal lobe. As you are in a heightened emotional state and you are engaging your frontal lobe, you have now activated a pathway in your emotional intelligence area.

Emotional Intelligence Area

Emotional intelligence is balanced between the limbic system and your frontal lobe. When you are feeling intense emotions, you must engage the frontal lobe and make the right decision. This decision must consider the long-term or short-term impact of all parties involved. As you continue to make these tough decisions in intense emotion, your emotional health will grow stronger and stronger. Unfortunately, many of us have not developed the skill set needed to provide a healthier response. As a result, toxic behavior will continue. If you continue to abort the mission and not allow emotions to subside, your emotional health will always be in the same place. You must decide in the heat of the moment to speak softer, or not speak at all, to walk away, or to ask for forgiveness. These actions are not easy but making these decisions increases your emotional maturity and creates healthier relationships.

PUTTING IT ALL TOGETHER

Let's imagine all these areas when faced with a real-life situation. Imagine you are driving your car, and you are feeling relaxed and happy as you head to your destination. Suddenly, a truck pulls in front of you, and you must slam on brakes to avoid running directly into him. Go back to Diagram 1 as our reference point for this exercise. Write down what information was coming in through your five senses.

SIGHT – What did your physical eyes see as the truck jumped in front of you?

_____

_____

SOUND – What sounds did you hear?

_____

_____

TOUCH – What were you touching?

_____

_____

SMELL – What did you smell?

_____

_____

TASTE – Did you taste anything?

_____

_____

All that information that came in through your senses happened in milliseconds and now you are feeling some type of way. What emotions do you feel when the truck unexpectedly cuts you off?

HEARTWORK OF THE SOUL

_____

_____

While you are feeling some type of way (feeling angry, irritated, frustrated, etc.), your emotions are telling you that you must do something about the problem at hand. What have you done in the present or past, or as a result of demanding emotions?

_____

_____

Did you decide to drive faster and cut them off, curse, yell, pray (for some people), etc. from your limbic system or your frontal lobe? That decision came from your limbic system. Now what if you decided to yell at the other driver, found out they were having a horrible day, and they decided you were going to pay for irritating them that day? Things immediately escalated, and a fight began. Did you give serious consideration to the long-term consequences of your decision? Unfortunately, when we decide without engaging the frontal lobe, we become emotionally hijacked. Many relationships have failed, jobs have been lost, families broken, etc. because of emotional hijacking. We are simply unaware in the heat of the moment that we need to pivot. However, there is another way, but it takes HeartWork®.

Our emotions directly impact other parts of our body other than the brain. Research in East Asian medicine[12] dove into the impact of our emotions on internal organs (See Diagram A2).

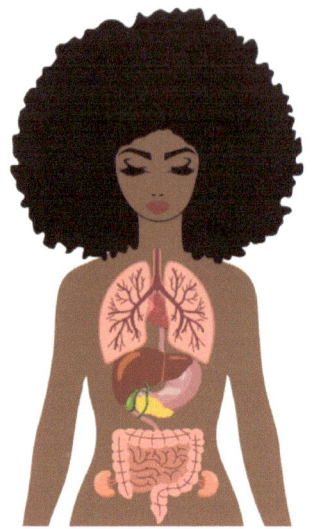

Imbalances in emotions can lead to illnesses in their corresponding organs.

LUNGS	LIVER	KIDNEYS	HEART	INTESTINES	GALLBLADDER
Anxiety Sadness	Anger Fear	Fear	Anxiety Fear Happiness Sadness Surprise Thoughtfulness	Fear Anxiety Worry	Fear Surprise

Diagram A2

If you take a look at the organs and their corresponding emotions, you will see the following. Anger is related to the liver, happiness to the heart, thoughtfulness to the heart and spleen, sadness to the heart and lungs, fear to the kidneys, heart, liver, and gallbladder, surprise to the heart and the gallbladder, and anxiety to the heart and the lungs. Imbalances in emotions can lead to illnesses or disease[13].

Did you notice that the heart is the organ most impacted by our emotions? It's no surprise that heart disease is one of the top causes of death in the United States[14]. Fortunately, many heart diseases can be regulated by incorporating healthier practices into the body such as clean eating, exercise, proper rest, and expressing emotions as needed. Unfortunately, many people have adopted societal and cultural norms that are killing them from the inside out. Awareness and intentionality to incorporate better practices concerning your health is pivotal in maintaining a healthier body.

REVIEW: ARE YOU FEELING SOME TYPE OF WAY?

1. Our brain is designed to default on _____ initially.
2. Information from our _____ enters our brain through the _____ _____.
3. This area of our brain stores our emotions and memories. _____
4. Our _____ is responsible for our rational thinking. This area of our brain allows us to think about the long- and short-term consequences of our behavior.
5. This organ of the body is the most impacted by our emotions. _____

Key Notes From Chapter

- According to *Psychology Today*, it is said that emotions drive 80 percent of the choices Americans make, while practicality and objectivity only represent about 20 percent of decision making.

- Research by Dr. Travis Bradberry indicated that only 34 percent of the time are we able to recognize and identify what we are feeling in the moment. This indicates that an estimated 46 percent of the time we are making decisions based on how we feel in the moment without realization.

- Decisions that are made that have not been processed by the frontal lobe lead to emotionally hijacked decisions. These decisions may cause damage to oneself or others.

- Emotions impact our internal organs, and long-term suppression can lead to cardiovascular issues.

- Commit to taking the HeartWork® Challenges for improved emotional wellness.

PART II

Are You Babysitting Spinach?

You are having dinner at a restaurant and after you have completed your meal you begin to engage in conversation with everyone seated at the table. Conversation flows very well, and your friend is motioning to you that you may have something in your teeth. You rub your tongue across your teeth to locate the food. After several attempts you assume you have cleared the food and continue in conversation. Thirty minutes later, you excuse yourself to go to the restroom. After using the restroom, you proceed to wash your hands and take a last glance in the mirror. As you look at your reflection you notice there is a large green leaf of spinach stuck between your teeth. You are mortified and you begin to wonder how long it has been stuck there. You begin thinking about your friends and family at the table. You don't recall anyone motioning or informing you that the leaf was still present. Has this happened to you before? Maybe it wasn't a spinach leaf, maybe you dragged toilet tissue out of a restroom on the bottom of your shoe or found out how your actions in a meeting required an additional meeting without your presence. These are embarrassing moments that - if we had a level of self-awareness - we may have adjusted correctly and immediately. Unfortunately, many times we go through life with spinach in our teeth. The upsetting thing about it all is that family, friends, coworkers, etc. have communicated these areas of opportunities or spinach repeatedly. Many times, we allow stubbornness, pride, or our ego to dictate our actions and we choose not to make the necessary changes. Thus, we go through life not fully embracing self-development and we become liabilities to everyone. *Maturity is not just knowing things but applying the things you know; growth happens at that place.* Self-Awareness begins this application process.

SELF-AWARENESS

According to Daniel Goleman, self-awareness is the ability to recognize and understand our moods, emotions, drivers as well as their effects on ourselves and others[15]. Dr. Tasha Eurich, a psychologist, researcher, and best-selling author completed a study discussed in a 2018 article in The Harvard Business Review. The research showed that although 90 to 95 percent of people believe they are self-aware, only 10 to 15 percent actually fit the criteria[16]. I was floored when I initially read this study. As I studied and became trained in emotional intelligence, I saw the disconnect between participants' self-actualization and feedback of themselves that they received from family, friends, coworkers, and peers within the class. At this point, I knew this was at the root of many stagnancies in peoples' lives and I saw it within my life. I had to begin to do the HeartWork® to understand my attitudes and behaviors. I can recall a period in my life when I was training 80 percent of the day at work. Without realizing that, when I walked in my front door my three kids (all under five) were expecting me to attend to them. I found myself irritated and short with them when they simply wanted to spend time with me. A few weeks went by and one day when I walked into the house, no one was there to greet me. The next day the same thing happened, and it continued. I began asking myself if I was to blame for the lack of attention from my kids.

I realized that training for six to eight hours a day left me depleted and I needed to recharge before I engaged with my family. I was able to finally recognize my mood and the emotions driving my actions. I communicated with my kids that I would need a few minutes to recharge and then I would give them all the attention they needed. This new attitude completely changed how I interacted with my children after a long day at work and I was no longer the angry mom. I no longer allowed my workday to dictate my relationship with my family.

Isn't it amazing that we suppress our emotions, wear a fake smile, be intentional about listening, pay attention to how we communicate, etc. for our coworkers but won't demonstrate those behaviors to the people who love us the most? We suppress many of our emotions during the day at work, so by the time we get home we are ticking time bombs for everyone around us. We unleash our fury and never realize that it wasn't what your husband said, or what your child said, or what your wife said that got you angry. It was the suppressed frustration that you did not let out in the meeting or conversation with your supervisor. We take things out on the people that will have our backs when the job decides to let us go. The people who will stop what they are doing to tend to us when we have a medical emergency. The people that have been there for us through all the highs and the lows. These are the ones we consistently overlook in our behavior. We must do better, however many of us are unaware when we are doing it or don't have the vocabulary to articulate our state of mind. So, how do we gain awareness when we are operating from an unconscious state of emotions?

EMOT-SUN® VOCABULARY

Previously we learned that an estimated 50 percent of the time we make decisions on autopilot. One of the first things we must be intentional about is identifying our current state of mind. Unfortunately, many are not aware of the emotional vocabulary for expression. The Emot-Sun® Diagram, (Diagram A3) provides an array of additional emotions that we experience but rarely communicate.

In the middle of the Emot-Sun® are our six primitive emotions. We touched on these emotions earlier in the text. Although these emotions arise spontaneously, our upbringing, culture, gender, etc. has shaped our ability to express them. When we are faced with external stimuli, (because we don't have the skill of identifying and articulating what we are experiencing), we leave it up to others to guess what we are feeling. It is much like you responding to the doctor's inquiry about symptoms you are experiencing by asking them to guess what kind of symptoms you are having. Or like you giving them incorrect symptoms because you can't identify what you're truly experiencing. How will the doctor be able to diagnose or assist you? This is the same demand that we are requiring of others and this practice does a disservice to you and the other party. So, what should we do?

The Emot-Sun® Diagram provides vocabulary to express how you are feeling for accuracy. For example, in conflict you may be exuding or demonstrating the energy of anger. The person you are in conflict with begins to respond to you based on that energy and demonstration. However, what if you are not angry and the emotion that you are feeling is hurt? They expressed something that hurt you and you felt disappointed that they responded to you in that manner. If you articulated your true emotions, do you think they would respond differently, most likely they would? Responding to someone that is hurt and responding to someone that is angry will be different. Unfortunately, since we are unable to identify our true emotions, we leave people in the dark because we are in the dark.

The Emot-Sun® Diagram provides additional verbiage that will help communication and provide a sense of clarity in discussions. Communication is effective when ideas and emotions are shared or exchanged. Often, we speak to people from logic but do not include the emotions that come from our heart. The disregard to include emotions in conversations drives a transactional exchange. The conversation is lacking the flow of energy that helps to bring connection to each other. As a result, many leave conversations disconnected and confused by the exchange. My challenge to you is lean into those moments, no matter how difficult it seems. Fear is a major contributor to fragmented conversations and is the main reason we run from certain conversations.

Many people are afraid to articulate their emotions and express vulnerability. They may feel that if they express from that state of being, others will take advantage of them. However, this thought is a complete lie. Why? Articulating the heart brings truth and ultimately freedom to oneself. Unfortunately, many decide to suppress and disregard the underlying energy that is brewing on the inside. This undercurrent ultimately will begin to drive our moods and thoughts subconsciously. One of the most effective ways to experience freedom in our emotions is articulating them since emotions cannot be destroyed, only transferred, or converted. Emotions must be expressed, or they will begin to create pockets in your soul that will ultimately recycle pain and abuse to oneself and others. In other words, we will transfer those emotions over to others.

TRANSFERRING EMOTIONS

Have you ever heard the saying "misery loves company?" We have all experienced moments where we were having a great day; then we receive a call from someone we care about, and they unleash what has frustrated them or irritated them. The more they share the more our positive state of mind begins to shift. Before we realize it, we are now feeling frustrated and irritated and now they are off the phone. They have transferred their energy over to you. How do you avoid giving people access to your soul and replacing your joy with grief? Allow me to share three strategies. Be aware of other's emotions during conversations. Then choose if you would like to stay in joy or absorb their energy. If you choose joy, you must articulate to them that you notice where their energy is, and they have to either calm down or the conversation can get revisited at another time. Or you can allow them to choose to remain in a negative space and ultimately end up frustrated and irritated. Many times, we are unaware that people are choosing our state of mind. We have to get to the place where we are intentional about protecting our emotional health. The other way in which we choose our emotional state is by choosing to convert the emotion.

CONVERTING EMOTIONS

Have you ever been in a situation where you needed to have a tough conversation with someone that could impact your relationship? How did you feel after the conversation? You see, when one chooses to speak from a place of vulnerability, disgust, loneliness, or other emotions that energy is converted in real time. The person receiving the message feels the other person's strength. After the conversation, the person that initiated the conversation feels the weight lifted from the suppression, and feels love, power, and freedom. These attributes only come from difficult exchanges. You must choose power although you may feel vulnerable, after the exchange, the power will come. You must choose to love, in spite of how family, friends, and others may have treated you, so you can experience a level of freedom from fear. I understand that this is not an easy thing to do, however normally what is good for us comes with a process. No one plants a seed and expects a harvest the next day. That seed must first grow down in the darkness, break, expand, and then begin to sprout. Many of us expect to see results after a few days but life doesn't work that way. In order for a plant to experience growth it must receive the necessary nutrients from water and the sun. If the plant only received the sun, it would burn and ultimately die and if the plant only received water, it would ultimately die. Growth happens when a balanced amount of rain and water is provided. Growth happens when you choose vulnerability to receive power. Which will you choose?

HeartWork® Challenge

Think about some difficult conversations that you've had in the past. Use the Emot-Sun® Diagram and identify what you felt prior to the conversation and discover how you felt after the conversation. Write your responses below.

Emotions prior to
conversation: _____

Emotions after
conversation: _____

What did you learn about yourself through this activity and how will you show up differently, when presented with this challenge again?

_____
_____
_____

SELF-ASSESSMENT

Awareness also includes recognizing, identifying, and understanding how you show up and affect others every day. We discussed how to identify our emotions and now we must seek to understand how we are showing up. Psychologist Dr. Travis Bradberry completed a study that indicates that only 34 percent of the time are we able to identify and recognize what we are feeling in the moment. Increasing that percentage takes a deeper level of patience and commitment. So, where do you start? I'm glad you asked. Do you know your strengths and limitations? Have you taken an honest look at your patterns in your friendships, partners, work colleagues, etc.? One of the statements that I consistently heard growing up was that "birds of a feather flock together." Even in the criminal justice system if you were riding in a stolen car with a friend and you got pulled over, you may face the same charges as the friend who actually stole the vehicle. This doesn't seem fair but who you associate with speaks volumes about your character. So, how are you showing up in life and are you allowing other people to dictate your future?

Have you recognized how your upbringing, culture, religion, or trauma has shaped your value and belief system? I'm going to challenge you to begin this process of understanding yourself.

HeartWork® Challenge: Write down three strengths and three areas of opportunity in your character.

STRENGTHS

_____
_____
_____

AREAS OF OPPORTUNITY

_____
_____
_____

Next, ask a family member, friend, and a co-worker to list three strengths and three areas of opportunity for you.

FAMILY MEMBER

_____
_____
_____

FRIEND

_____
_____
_____

CO-WORKER

_____
_____
_____

Look at the feedback that you received from your family and friends and locate any consistent areas in your strengths and opportunities. After you have identified those areas, look at the feedback that you wrote concerning yourself. Was there consistency between the feedback that you provided for yourself and the feedback from your family and friends, and if not, what were the areas that were inconsistent? These areas indicate the spinach that you may have missed or have not made the necessary adjustments in your character. Write those areas down for future work.

_____
_____
_____

TRIGGERS

Now that you have a deeper understanding of your character, I'm going to challenge you again. Self-awareness also requires having a level of patience to dig into places within yourself that may be uncomfortable. Part of the definition of self-awareness is having a level of awareness concerning your triggers or drivers. A trigger is something that someone can do or say that can immediately cause you to feel an intense emotion. The intensity of this emotion can cause you to say or do things quickly without thinking about the short- or long-term impacts of your behavior. So, let's explore this together.

HEARTWORK OF THE SOUL

HeartWork® Challenge: Think about a trigger that can immediately cause you to get angry, sad, depressed, etc. and write it down.

TRIGGER: _____

I also want you to begin the drill down process of finding the root of this trigger. How do you find the root? Begin to ask yourself why and what may have caused this attitude. For example, you have identified that when people lie to you, you immediately feel frustrated, irritated, and angry. Ask yourself why do you get so angry? What is causing those feelings? What is the first memory that you can think of in which someone older lied to you and you couldn't do anything about it, so you suppressed the emotion? Was that person your mother, father, sibling, extended family? Think through these thoughts and be patient with yourself to allow the memories and feelings to resurface. You will probably begin to feel the same emotions that you were feeling in the memory and that is okay. Take a few moments to begin to analyze your memories. Have you identified the person that is at the seed of the trigger?

Write that name down _____

This exercise gives you an awareness of how childhood events can dictate how you treat others in the present. For example, let's say that you identified that your dad was at the root of your trigger because he constantly lied to you when he told you that he would pick you up, or attend your extracurricular activities. Your anger may have turned inward and caused bitterness or resentment. Now when anyone lies to you, you have that same feeling about them. You begin demonstrating the characteristics of your father based on your trigger. That is a humbling thought and requires a level of acceptance and commitment to change. That requires the significant work of self-regulation.

As you have read, self-awareness is a journey and requires intentionality and patience. One must be dedicated to their personal or professional development. We will now cover a few essentials that will equip you through this journey, however you must have a level of commitment to yourself.

SELF-AWARENESS STRATEGIES

1. *Pay attention to your emotions.* Anytime you encounter something or someone and they say or do something that causes you to feel an intense emotion, make a mental note to explore it later. Your emotions are an alert that some HeartWork® is required in this area. You must create the time to find a quiet place, grab a journal, and sit with your thoughts. Allow the details of the incident to flood your thoughts and begin asking yourself a few questions. What was the emotion that you were feeling (use the Emot-Sun Wheel)? What are the thoughts that may be driving those emotions, and is it connected to a childhood memory? Asking these questions allows you to begin to dig into your soul to see what may be out of place. Attention to these emotions is critical since they can become chronic and lead to illnesses in your body or mind.
2. *Study yourself.* Think about your culture, upbringing, religion, life experiences, etc. These areas have shaped who you are and your biases. Understand that all people were not raised like you, do not have the same culture, or religion, etc. Which means that we all must be intentional

and open minded when learning about other people. Many times, we feel our perspective is the right perspective, or trumps other perspectives, and that is not true. Your perspective is just that – your perspective.

When you find yourself in conflict with someone, use this as an opportunity to learn about the history of others. Understanding the history of others will give insight on how you should conduct yourself. Ask them where they learned or got that perspective? How was that perspective fed by oneself or others? These questions open the door by adding context. Don't make the mistake of thinking a problem can be solved with two clues; it takes more than what is presented to make an informed decision.

3. *Establish a safe community around you.* Seeking counsel is vital to emotional development. Select friends and family who will be honest with you and speak to you with love and kindness. These individuals can inform you when you are operating out of balance and out of character. It is important to receive their words without defense or judgment. Understand you placed them in that position because they care for you and think good thoughts about you. Embracing this circle will provide a check and balance on a daily basis and help your awareness grow deeper.

Self-awareness is a process that will continually prove itself to you. Naturally, we develop every day. We don't think or look the way that we did when we were five years old or when we were fifteen years old. We are gradually growing mentally and physically. Embracing this journey of self-discovery will allow you to grow emotionally. One's development in life shouldn't just pertain to where they are physically or mentally but also emotionally. The

EQ stats that were discussed earlier alluded to the escalation of success for those who are emotionally well. Self-awareness allows you to not skim past the spinach in your teeth but get up, look in the mirror, grab a flosser and be thorough to ensure no green leaves remain.

TESTIMONY CORNER

Jerry attended one of my emotional intelligence classes and was very enthusiastic about it. On the first day, Jerry came on heavy and strong in his demeanor. He was very opinionated, forceful, and prideful in many of his statements. Many of his perspectives were based out of trauma, culture, or upbringing. As I began to shed light on a few of his perspectives he became defensive and irritated. He was raised with many common misconceptions: showing emotions makes you weak, his perspective was the right perspective, women are more emotional than men, etc. Throughout the course I debunked a lot of these beliefs with emotional intelligence evidence. However, the new information was challenging for him to embrace. He made sure through the four-day training to voice his counter opinions at every opportunity. I welcomed the challenge since I knew that emotional intelligence is not an easy skill set to accept.

Jerry completed the training, passed the assessment, and moved on to another phase of his training. I no longer had contact with him. Two weeks after the class, Jerry reached out to me on Facebook with this message. *"My name is Jerry and I just wanted to thank you for all that you did for me. A few days before our class I was in the worst place of my life. I didn't realize I was there because I was stubborn, and I overestimated myself in things I knew very little about. During our class you really showed me a lot. It's like you put my body on autopilot and took my soul out of my body to show myself how I reflect everyone around me. The experience was amazing. A light bulb turned on in my head during the training. I feel like you saved me from myself. I didn't realize how the energy I put out was affecting people and that led me to a very dark and lonely place in my life. For you to have the ability to reach out and save me from myself is a different talent. I don't think it's a talent, it's just something that you were blessed with and I'm really thankful for meeting you. You changed my life in a way that no one has done before and I'm very thankful. You gave me a layout to guide me through life from a different perspective and I will continue to grow and evolve in my thinking. I just wanted to stop by and say thank you."*

After reading his message I was blown away by his transparency and honesty. Jerry gained awareness of how he was showing up in life and began to take responsibility for his actions. He finally got up to go to the bathroom, look in the mirror, and be intentional about removing the spinach leaf from his teeth. Hopefully, you will begin to take inventory of your thoughts and beliefs and recognize that you create the world that you want to see.

REVIEW: ARE YOU BABYSITTING SPINACH?

1. Research shows that although 90 to 95 percent of people believe they are self-aware, _____ to _____ percent actually fit the criteria.
2. Increasing that percentage takes a deeper level of understanding, patience, and _____.
3. According to your HeartWork® Challenge Assessment, which areas were consistent from the feedback that you received from your family, friend, and co-worker?

_____
_____
_____

According to your HeartWork® Challenge Assessment, identify and write the areas that were consistent with your (family, friends, co-worker) feedback that did not align with the feedback that you wrote about yourself.

4. _____
   _____
   _____

5. Which area will you be more intentional about correcting?

_____
_____
_____

Key Notes From Chapter

- *Maturity is not just knowing things but applying the things you know; growth happens at that place.* Self-Awareness begins this application process.

- *Pay attention to your emotions.* Anytime you encounter something or someone and they say or do something that causes you to feel an intense emotion, make a mental note to explore this later.

- *Study yourself.* Think about your culture, upbringing, religion, life experiences, etc. These areas have shaped who you are and your biases.

- *Establish a safe community around you.* Seeking counsel is vital to emotional development. Select friends and family who will be honest with you and speak to you with love and kindness.

- Self-awareness allows you to not simply skim past the spinach in your teeth but get up, look in the mirror, grab a flosser and be thorough to ensure no green leaves remain.

PART III

Get It Togetha

I remember when I used to get in trouble as a child (for doing something I had no business doing), my mom would tell me that I needed to get it togetha or she would get it togetha for me (and you must read that with a little bit of attitude). When I was younger, I had trouble understanding what she meant but I eventually caught on. She was telling me that I needed to manage what I was feeling and not make a fool out of myself or her. We have all been in situations where we behaved in a way that didn't reflect our best. Unfortunately, many of us realized that behavior after the damage was done. Feelings of guilt, shame, or remorse, etc. flooded our thoughts because we knew we should have been better. As a result of that realization, we apologize and seek forgiveness from the person whom we may have harmed. What if I told you there is a healthy way to remove that foot from your mouth prior to you placing it there?

SELF-REGULATION

I learned early that I needed to get myself together prior to events happening. It wasn't until my exposure to emotional intelligence; I fully understood this principle. Many people look to control themselves at the moment and they feel that they have done a good thing. Unfortunately, this pattern of behavior will continue because you haven't gotten to the root of the emotion. Daniel Goleman defines self-regulation as the ability to manage disruptive emotions and impulses, and to think before you react.[17] Think about a volcano for a moment. What do you envision, what do you hear, what do you see? Many people associate volcanoes with heat, fire, lava, eruption, pressure, explosion, etc. However, hours, or even minutes before an eruption, earthquakes and tremors occur. This can be viewed as an alert for people to evacuate or seek safety. If you are unable to get into a safe place you can be severely injured. Now, I want you to think about your emotions. Many times, we have been alerted by life experiences that we have areas within us that we need to evaluate and clean up. One person's area may be stubbornness, another anger, another unforgiveness, etc. Regardless of the area there must be a level of intentionality to get to the root of the emotion. Our emotions can act as a tremor or earthquake trying to warn us that an explosion is on its way. Unfortunately, we may suppress or be intentional about not addressing the red flags. Then, an unsuspecting bystander does one thing that pushes our button, and they become the target of our eruption; how unfair. Some of us even blame them for pushing our buttons. Always keep in mind that *people can't push buttons that you don't present.* If they can push your button, then they have power over you at any moment. I learned this reluctantly in my personal experiences. I realized that I should've been better and managed my emotions prior to the moment of eruption. I also realized that I had become enslaved to their reactions. I felt powerless and finally understood that if I stayed in that state of mind, I was a slave to them mentally and emotionally. I needed to be better. Being better began when I started to understand that my thoughts or the narratives that I created needed some direction and intentionality.

MANAGING NEGATIVE THOUGHTS

Managing disruptive thoughts, emotions, and impulses takes HeartWork®. This work is not easy and requires an open mind and attentiveness to the process. One major contaminant to becoming free of obtrusive and harmful thoughts is our self-talk. Several types of self-talk have been researched, but I am going to discuss four types that I have personally experienced.

1. Brain Reading: You assume that you know what people are going to think, even though you don't have enough evidence about their thoughts.

2. Fortune-telling: You think you can predict the future and that everything will be worse or something dangerous will happen.

3. Labeling: You have subconscious negative opinions about yourself or others. You claim that the positive things you or others have been are insignificant.

4. Negative filter: You'll focus on anything negative that could happen. You become so consumed by this narrative that you build damaging thoughts, forgetting that good could come out of the situation.

HeartWork® Challenge

If you had all the financial resources that were needed, already acquired the necessary education, time was not an issue, and physically you were in good shape, what is one of your ambitions?

Write it _____

If I challenged you to begin strategizing to manifest that dream today, what thoughts would hinder you?

Thoughts _____
_____
_____

Look at the thoughts that you wrote down. Do they fall into one of the self-talk categories? If they do that simply means that the thought of your hindrance is rooted in fear. These four types of self-talk focus on the unknown or impossibility of a positive outcome. These thoughts do not consider the power of hope or faith in a person or situation. Fear creates figments of your imagination that can lead you to paralysis in your actions or abort the dreams that you created. You will hear me refer to fear as a liar or lie, since it's a false representation of your future. The more you listen to these lies the more you will stay stagnant in your thoughts and eventually your behaviors. We discussed earlier that emotions drive eighty to ninety percent of your decision making. The way that you think is going to impact how you feel and how you feel will dictate what you do (Think. Feel. Do).

DREAM AGAIN

I encourage you to reconsider the dream or ambition that you wrote previously and don't allow any negative thoughts to impede your progress. If you have a desire to write a book, go to school, have children, get married, own a home, etc. Whatever you want to pursue, pursue it with tenacious faith and courage. Faith sees what you're hoping for and gives you a vision. After you have decided to move in faith, courage says get up and start moving. Start researching the details for writing a book, begin looking at homes, start researching schools, etc. Get others involved but only share with family or friends who are positive and hopeful. Some people are called dream killers because they provide advice based on their failed attempts and now, they want you to join in their misery. Don't fall for it.

GET IT TOGETHA STRATEGIES

So, let's "get it togetha" and start moving. Here are a few strategies that will help you break the cycle of disruptive or volcanic eruptions.

1. *Manage your negative thoughts.* The average human brain has over 70,000 thoughts per day and 80% of these thoughts are negative. There is also evidence that 90% of all thoughts are repetitive[18]. If you constantly think negative thoughts, your life will ultimately reflect those thoughts. King Solomon, whose story unfolds in the Old Testament of The Holy Bible said, "As a man thinks in his heart, so is he." Chinese Philosopher Lao Tuz said, "Watch your thoughts; they become words. Watch your words; they become actions. Watch your actions; they become a habit. Watch your habits; they become character. Watch your character; it becomes your destiny."

Ultimately, we are a product of our thoughts and moods. How can we counteract these patterns of thinking? You must attack the false thoughts and replace them with what is true. If you have a thought that says, "you're not good enough," replace that thought with affirming words. Speak aloud, "you are good enough", rinse and repeat until you convince yourself that you are. I like to say, "faith it 'til you make it." Remove words like always, never, and every. Replace them with hopeful words such as "I'm going to try," "I got through something similar before," or "I'm going to call a friend for good counsel." *Thoughts are powerless until you begin to believe them and give them life by picking them apart.* You have a choice: whether you will succumb to your thoughts and allow them to dictate your life or choose to speak what's true and hopeful. I hope you make the right choice.

2. *Focus on the things that you can control.* I recall a time when I was in a deficit financially; we were in the middle of a pandemic, and I could no longer drive for Uber and Lyft to support my living. I remember thinking things couldn't get worse and then we received a three-day eviction notice. I felt overwhelmed, powerless, and like an unfit parent since I was subjecting my kids to this fate. Then I began to think, this is not the first time finances were tight in my life, and we made it through. Gratefully, I was not sick, nor was my family ill because of the pandemic. I couldn't drive then, but I could receive unemployment benefits from the state. Issue by issue, I began thinking about the part that I had control over, and I also thought of a quote that said, *"You have survived one hundred percent of your worst days."* I decided to take things one day at a time. As I write, I think about the song the old folks used to sing, One day at a time, *sweet Jesus*. Things were going to get better, but I was going to have to ride out the storm until it passed. The only thing that I was going to focus on was what I could control. Eventually, everything worked out, and I learned a valuable lesson. No matter what you are experiencing through your five senses or

what you're feeling in the moments, as my Pastor, Bishop Henry Fernandez of The Faith Center (Florida), would say, *"Every problem has an expiration date."*

3. *Discover and understand your triggers.* Earlier (in Part II), you were able to identify one trigger and you were able to get to the seed of the trigger. Continue this journey with other things or people that tend to set you off. Never allow the emotional reaction of someone else to dictate your response or actions. I learned this extremely hard lesson. I would not communicate how I felt because I was afraid of how people would respond. I learned that when you close your mouth you are saying that the other person's comfort level is more valuable than you. Is that true? Does their comfort trump how you are feeling? Absolutely NOT! Say what you need to say in love and with kindness and however they choose to respond, that's on them. Don't make yourself the babysitter of their emotions. Also, don't allow someone to drive you to act out of who you know you are. Remember, *people can only push the buttons that you present.* If you clean up the trigger, those keys will no longer be available. We give other people too much power over our speech and behaviors. After we have behaved out of character, we wonder how we allowed ourselves to react in that manner. We can't control others, but we can always control how we behave. Be intentional about not allowing someone to transfer their energy over to you.

HEALING THE SOUL

Getting it togetha, also requires completing some HeartWork®. Healing the soul is pivotal to your emotional wellness. I challenged you earlier to identify the person at the seed of your trigger. We are now going to drill down a bit deeper. For healing to begin you can no longer suppress what you have been feeling. *Remember emotions cannot be destroyed, only transferred, or converted.* Intentionality must be put in place for your soul to experience the healing. The next HeartWork® challenge will provide the specifics for you to begin the work.

HeartWork® Challenge

Each time I get to teach EI, I challenge participants to begin the process of healing their triggers. Below are steps that will empower you to release the energy that can ultimately cause damage to you internally.

1. *Write a letter*. In Part II, you worked through getting to the seed of your trigger. Grab a pen and paper or a device that can capture your thoughts. Recall the memory that caused an emotion to emerge. Sit with yourself and begin to write down your thoughts and express the areas in which you were unable to release previously. Use the Emo-Sun Wheel to identify and articulate the emotions that will arise. Explain in the letter how their actions impact your behaviors as an adult. Use this as an opportunity to get it all out, in love and with kindness.

2. *Forgive yourself and the seed of your trigger. Forgiveness is one of the keys that unlocks the hardness of the heart.* Forgiveness

also releases the emotions that have been explosive when your buttons are pushed. Many times, we think that if we forgive people, we are letting them off the hook, and they need to pay for what they did to us. However, forgiveness does not let them off the hook but lets you off the hook to live a healed life.

3. *Read the letter to the seed of your trigger.* This is a tremendously difficult step. I've heard of people trying to manage unforgiveness by making a list of the people that they need to forgive and saying, "I forgive you," to each name listed. Unfortunately, this strategy does not convert or transfer the internal energy. Allowing yourself to go back to the memory, feel the emotion, and speak while expressing the emotion allows for a healthy conversion. You may not be able to forget the memory but doing the HeartWork® enables you to redeem the memory. The stench of the pain and hurt will be replaced with a peace that comes through your forgiveness. I'm going to challenge you to read your letter to the person at the root of your seed. This is where the negative thoughts will begin to overwhelm your mind. The mission of those thoughts is to keep you in internal pain, but don't give in. Reading the letter converts the stored energy that you are feeling (weak, anxious, or insecure) and allows you to feel strengthened, encouraged, and relieved.

4. *If the seed of your trigger is deceased,* complete the first two steps. The only difference is that you will read your letter to a proxy that will stand in the gap for the deceased individual. Choose someone that you trust and thinks good thoughts about you. Set a time and date and release your words.

I understand that this assignment is difficult and that is why it's HeartWork®. Things of the heart will take soul work. I completed the assignment because of the daddy issues that I had growing up. My dad died when I was about seven. I suffered with abandonment, low self-esteem, fear of rejection and other things that I couldn't identify. When I completed this assignment, it felt like a 50-pound weight was lifted off my shoulders. Every person that took heed to the challenge has experienced transformational change in their life. You deserve to be free, but you must take the first step.

LETTER EXPECTATIONS

I'm glad you are going to take on this challenge. Now let me set you up with some realistic expectations concerning this conversation.

1. Do not expect them to apologize, acknowledge, or validate the information that you have shared. You have had repetitive thoughts concerning them, but they had no idea how you felt. It will take time for them to process things and they may initially become defensive. Don't fall into the trap or give them that power over you. Take a deep breath, slow your speech, and continue to share what was in your heart.

2. Do not expect reconciliation. Reconciliation only happens when both parties have heard, understood, and have taken acceptance and accountability for their actions. Once resolve is achieved from both sides, future reconciliation is possible.

3. Expect the emotional weight that was on your heart to feel lighter. Take note of how your confidence and strength will develop. The triggers that used to hold you bound you have now developed a level of awareness and it's easier for you to decide to do the right thing.

TESTIMONY CORNER

Leroy Darden, my dad, was a man of God who traveled to different countries to open eleven churches. He was on the mission field most of my life but when he came home, I remember feeling excited and energized. I was about three to five years old at the time, and he was like a giant to me. He was six feet four inches tall, and he would pick me up and swing me through the air like an airplane. I remember feeling so high off the ground but also so secure. My mom is about five feet, so her picking me up was completely different. Nevertheless, when he came home, life was different. He was very playful, and my siblings and I were always doing things to fight for his attention.

I remember hearing the news one day from my mom that he wasn't coming back home. He was in a city in Florida ministering. After service, he left the church and proceeded to cross a street, he was immediately struck by a car. At six how do you manage hearing or understanding that your father is never coming back to hold you, protect you, or just be there for you? Growing up, I got into many fights with my siblings and other children because of unresolved anger. I didn't know that's what it was then. I also got into relationships for safety, protection, and stability. Why was a 16-year-old looking for another teenager to provide safety, protection, and stability? As a result of feeling powerless, alone, and abandoned, I began to make terrible decisions. I began dating people who didn't care about me but wanted me for what I could give them. I began to accept people not treating me as someone with value. These actions made me feel disgusted with myself. I hated who I had become. I remember after I had been with someone that I barely knew, I felt like an idiot. I walked away with so much shame and guilt. Unforgiveness was brewing so heavily in me, and I wasn't aware of it, so I couldn't self-regulate.

One day, as I was sitting with myself, I started to think about some of the decisions that I made as a teenager and as an adult, and I began to drill down to find the root of these actions. Doing the HeartWork®, I came to the awareness that I still suffered from abandonment trauma and unforgiveness from my father passing away. I knew I must regulate my actions because of this awareness, but how? In the self-regulation of EI, I encourage my students to write a letter to express their emotions. So, I wrote a letter to my father, read it to a close male friend of mine, who is also a minister, and chose to grow through the trauma. I'll never forget when we met at a park, and I pulled up a picture of my father on my phone. My minister friend held up the picture as I read. The more I read, the more I cried. I cried to the point where my eyes were swollen. I had been carrying so much weight in my soul that needed to be released. After I read the letter, I burned the paper and remembered feeling the 50-pound brick immediately released from my heart. After that day and until this day, that work created a window of awareness. Actions that I used to jump right into (because of the trauma), I now pause to choose my action. A window of grace was opened to allow me to see myself and others differently. Additionally, there was an awareness of my actions illuminated that I continue to benefit from. This is the power that comes with self-regulation and forgiveness.

REVIEW: GET IT TOGETHA

1. _____ is defined as the ability to manage disruptive emotions and impulses and to think before you react.
2. You assume that you know what people are going to think, even though you don't have enough evidence about their thoughts, this refers to _____ _____.
3. Whatever you want to achieve, pursue it with tenacious _____ and _____. Faith sees what you're hoping for and gives you a vision.
4. Remember, emotions cannot be destroyed, only _____ or converted.
5. Select an accountability partner, set a date to write your letter, and carry out the process of releasing those suppressed emotions. What date will you commit to? _____
_____

Key Notes From Chapter

- *People can't push buttons that you don't present.* If they can push your button, then they have power over you at that moment.

- Fear creates figments of your imagination that can lead you to paralysis in your actions or abort the dreams that you created. Fear is a false representation of your future. Don't believe the lies!

- The average human brain has over 70,000 thoughts per day [10] and the majority of these thoughts are negative.

There is evidence that 90 percent of all thoughts are repetitive.

- Forgiveness is one of the keys that unlocks the hardness of the heart. Forgiveness does not let them off the hook but lets you off the hook to live a healed life.

- Commit to taking the HeartWork® Letter Challenge and begin the process of healing your soul.

PART IV

Sick and Tired of Being Sick and Tired?

About a year after my second child, Brianna, was born, I decided enough was enough. I was sick and tired of being sick and tired. I told myself, "I must do something, and it must start now!" I was feeling super motivated, so I started my weight loss journey. I was excited, eager, and ready to jump in. I was hoping to lose at least 50 pounds and reduce my dress size from an 18 to a size 10. I began telling myself, "Jo, you got this." I started working out with a trainer, joined a nutrition program, and was on my way. About seven months in, I was down about 25 pounds and feeling ecstatic. My dress size went from 18 to 14; I was so confident. Suddenly, I started to feel unusually tired and nauseous, and it became harder for me to stick to my food regimen. These feelings felt familiar. The next morning, I quickly went to the store and purchased a pregnancy test. The test came back positive. What do you do when you have started that new project and the unexpected happens? Y'all I gotta be honest. I was upset and disappointed. All the work I had done seemed pointless. So, during that pregnancy, I ate, and ate, and ate, and then ate some more. I would drink a two-liter bottle of soda every other day. The day I entered the hospital to have my son Gabriel, I weighed 290 pounds (and I was two weeks early). When my son was four, I weighed myself again, and I was

270 pounds and wore a size 20 dress. I was back at that place of being sick and tired and could no longer say it was baby weight. My family started a biggest loser weight competition and that was the motivation that I needed to get started.

MOTIVATION

Motivation is defined as the general desire or willingness to do something[19]. I had a general desire to lose weight, and the biggest loser challenge was the boost I needed. If you ever owned a vehicle and had battery issues, you may be familiar with this situation. Every now and again, when your battery dies you need a jump to get you going again. I had a general desire to lose weight, so that desire became my jumpstart. The following Monday morning, after my family started our challenge, I got up at 4:30 am to head to the gym (you know how we like to start our get fit programs on Monday). Tuesday, I got up, Wednesday, I got up, and Thursday came, and that motivation that I was riding on from Monday died. My joints were hurting, I was exhausted from working a full-time job, taking care of three children, being in ministry, and being a wife. It was A LOT! What do you do when you have decided that you are going to try that project again, write that book, go to school, etc. and it seems like everything is now impeding your progress? *Discipline picks you up when motivation drops you off.* I realized that motivation is an emotion, a general desire and discipline was going to have to kick in to get me to the finish line.

Discipline is defined as control gained by enforcing obedience or order, demonstrating self-control[20]. I had to take full control over my situation and decide that my motherly duties, work, ministry, or being a wife were not going to dictate my health. I love that discipline does not rely on emotions; it is a choice. You must decide that you are going to follow a routine to get your desired results. Your progress is going to be measured by your level of commitment and perseverance through your journey. Unfortunately, many of us fail to meet our goals because we are simply not disciplined in our actions. Discipline takes intentionality and much patience. The only person that can stop you from completing your goals is yourself. The battle begins between your ears first. How do we win the war that begins within ourselves? You must take initiative, set your goals, be committed to the process, and embrace the fears that will arise on your journey.

TAKING INITIATIVE

Wayne Gretsky said, "You miss 100% of the shots you don't take." If you never take the shot, if you never start the business, if you never start pursuing your goals, then you have already quit. A disciplined and dedicated runner does not buy the necessary gear to run a race such as sneakers, a hat, water, wristbands, etc., and never shows up for the race. Unfortunately, many of us have done that exact thing and ~~have~~ given up on ourselves before we even start. *Taking initiative is the power that will fuel your action* regardless of others. Too often, we rely on the approval or guidance from others to get started. If we rely on others for their input, we will always rely on them. This will also lead to our successes or failures being defined by others. Embracing that type of mentality will keep you enslaved to others. What if I told you that you already have what you need to get started. Would you believe me? During my weight loss journey, I began walking on the treadmill for cardio work. When I started walking, I would walk between four to four and a half miles per hour. I slowly increased it to five miles per hour and after only a few minutes of running I was exhausted. I thought I would never be able to run consistently at a faster pace. Later in my journey, I hit 11.0 miles per hour and began sprinting. I could not believe after running to the maximum speed (of that particular treadmill) that I was capable of running at such a fast pace. I had the increased speed in me the entire time! I had to continue to take the initiative in my training and challenge myself. Taking the initiative of increasing my speed and duration of each run fueled the power in me to run a half marathon (13.1 miles). Three half marathons later, I determined that we can truly complete whatever we want in life, but we have to begin by putting the power behind our actions. After I took the initiative, I needed something else to refuel me since I wasn't at my weight loss goal. I began to understand that I needed to set clear short and long-term goals for my ultimate success.

SETTING GOALS

According to Reliable Plant, only 20 percent of people set goals for themselves. What's even more unfortunate is that out of the 20 percent of people who do set goals, only about 30 percent of them will succeed. Only a third of those people who set goals achieve them and of all people, which makes up six percent[21]. These numbers are an indicator that most people don't set goals, and the ones that set their goals, only a fraction of them will achieve their goal. How many times have you set a goal, written it down, and accomplished what you started? What hindered you? Sometimes, we can allow negative thoughts to dictate our actions. Whatever the reason, how do you get back on?

I shared that I was excited and felt motivated to begin my workout journey, and for the first four days of the week, I felt great, but gradually, I was losing steam. I decided ~~that~~ I would no longer allow circumstances to dictate my workout regimen. I was going to finish what I started. I had a goal in my mind that I would see to the end! *Change begins when you shift your attitude*. I couldn't afford to give up! I owed it to myself and to be around as long as possible for my family. A shift in my attitude was needed. Maybe you have relied on feeling motivated and gotten the same results from that type of thinking. It's time that you apply discipline and stick to your goals. You cannot continue to be available for everyone else but not yourself. You must make yourself a priority and find the time to take care of yourself to achieve your goals.

So, I got up every morning, about five days a week, and went to the gym. On Saturdays, I pushed myself even harder in the gym. The weight began to fall. Nine months into my disciplined mindset, I lost a total of 70 pounds and went from a dress size 20 to a size eight. Ten years later, I'm a size six and float between 180 to 185 pounds. I embraced the disciplined life and made up in my mind that I will never go back. I will always go to the gym like I will always eat fruits and vegetables. I decided that I would force my body to carry out what I wanted and not vice versa. My body didn't care that an unhealthy lifestyle would impact my longevity. It only cared about being comforted in the moment. If I gave in to my body's plan, I would have never achieved my goals. Are you giving in to your body's desires? Is your body dictating your actions? You must adopt a committed mindset in the process through your journey.

COMMITMENT TO YOUR PROCESS

Imagine that your child wants the newest electronic device for their birthday. Your spouse communicated what would make them happy for their birthday. Your friends also put their requests in for their wants. Although these wants can become overwhelming or challenging, many adults find a way to provide the specific requests of their child, spouse, or friend. We often make commitments to others many times without giving a second thought about what might be needed to meet the commitment. Even if we didn't have the resources, many of us would find a way to get our children what they want. Are you committed to your needs, endeavors, or dreams the way that you are committed to others? If you are honest with yourself, this is an area of opportunity for growth for each of us. We are so committed to others that we overlook our needs. Unfortunately, some maintain this mindset to keep from facing individual reality. Focusing on others is always a good distraction from paying attention to the areas that we need to develop and grow in. However, this way of thinking simply prolongs our growth, and we, in turn, may hurt others. Remember, hurt people hurt other people. Focusing on yourself is essential to your emotional maturity. Whenever you board an airplane, safety instructions are provided to the flier in case of an emergency. "Place your mask on yourself prior to placing the mask on anyone else, including your child," the flight attendant says. I remember flying and hearing that instruction years ago. I thought how selfish it would be to take care of myself prior to helping my child. However, the more I thought about the instruction, the more clarity was developed. How can I help my child or others if I can't breathe? However, if I place the mask on myself first then not only will I be able to assist my child, but possibly others in need. I decided to choose me and place the mask on first.

We need to have more of a commitment to ourselves and our dreams before considering others. This state of mind is not selfish, it is essential. Dedication to fulfilling your wants is the driving force that can catapult healthier relationships with yourself and others. When you are fulfilled, you show up differently. You're happier, empowered, and have a sense of freedom since you have prioritized yourself. Once you're prioritized you can fully commit to any process and see it to ~~its~~ completion. Whether that is writing a book, starting a new career, prioritizing self-care, etc., you have the power to conquer milestones. Many of us have attempted several goals but unfortunately, we get derailed in the process because of negative thoughts brewed in fear.

EMBRACE YOUR FEARS

Bishop TD Jakes, Founding Pastor of The Potter's House (TX), provides an acronym for fear: False, Evidence, Appearing, Real. Fear will paralyze your behaviors and actions by creating figments of the mind that you begin to believe. Let's take starting a business, for example. Many people have an entrepreneurial mindset. According to studies conducted by Zebra, a research organization, small businesses account for 1.5 million jobs annually and drive 44% of the economic activity in the United States. Although this is an encouraging statistic, fear will make you believe that you are not qualified, you won't make enough money for sustainability, there are already too many businesses that are similar to your business, etc. All these statements are simply not true unless you have psychic abilities and can see your future. However, we allow these thoughts to derail and stagnate our progress. I remember when I first had thoughts of starting my business. I woke up around three in the morning and heard the name of my business HeartWork®. I quickly wrote it down and pondered what products and services I would provide. I meditated on starting a business for weeks and as I began to conduct research on my competitors, I realized there are many people ~~that are~~ doing the same thing. I felt discouraged and began to question if I was qualified to start a business. I was married and had four children. Would I be able to sustain what I was earning in my corporate position? Facing those fears rattled me for some time, and then, one day at lunch, I spoke with a work colleague. He was established in his business and was doing well. He shared something with me that day that completely shredded all the fear that had paralyzed me for weeks. He said if you walk down the bread aisle, you will see an array of different types of bread. However, there are people who have experience with a particular brand, and they walk past all of the other breads to get to their preferred brand every time they go shopping. He shared that although there are many training and development companies, potential clients will choose my company because they LIKE ME! What he shared resonated in my heart so deeply. That day, I decided that after my season was up with my current position, I would never work for another corporation again. Two years after our conversation, I was laid off and used my severance pay to start my business. It has been one of the best decisions that I have made. Challenges occasionally plague the business, but I am committed to myself and will not allow any circumstances or fear to rob me of my destiny. What circumstances or fears have you allowed that have cut the life out of your dream? Decide in your heart and embrace that you will have failures on this journey, but you will never quit. You will push and push until your dream is established. This can be your reality if you establish discipline and take the first steps - taking the initiative, staying committed to the process, embracing all fears, and growing through them. You will end on top since you placed the oxygen mask over your face prior to anyone else's.

HeartWork® Challenge

Write three goals you would like to achieve and determine the steps that you must take to get to your desired result. For example, I had to commit to going to the gym, focus on my nutrition, and face the scale for accountability every week. What measures can you set up?

_____

_____

_____

DISCIPLINING YOURSELF STRATEGIES

I am glad that you have decided to shift your attitude. Allow nothing to stop you from achieving your goals. Below are a few strategies that can assist you on this journey.

1. *Awareness* – Identify the obstacles that prevented you from completing your goal previously. Drill down to understand the root reason and shift your attitude. Recognize the ways in which you can proactively address any barriers that caused a bottleneck previously. Recall the emotions that you felt when you decided that you were not going to go to the gym when you decided to embrace an unhealthy food option or anything that you were determined to accomplish, but you gave in to your emotions. If given another chance, would you make the same decision, and if so, why?

2. *Regulate - Set measurable goals with timelines and include an accountability partner.* Goals must be specific and attainable, including dates that coincide with each milestone. Often, we set goals and keep them in our heads. However, we will be more successful if we write the goals down. Ensure the goals that you have identified are attainable. For example, if your goal is to save $1,000 a month, you

must evaluate your monthly spending to ensure saving $1,000 is even possible. Lastly, set a date with each short- or long-term goal and share it with your accountability partner. They will help keep you on track with your timelines. Choose someone that you can trust and who will speak to you with love and kindness.

3. *Celebrate your results.* When was the last time you completed a goal and celebrated? We praise and buy for our children, family, and friends, and don't think twice. Sometimes we spend what we need to spend and count the cost later. How often do you practice this with yourself? Take the time and think of ways you can reward yourself after each milestone. Prioritize your wants and be proud of your accomplishments.

4. *Self-Assessment.* During the journey of achieving your goal, set a time to re-evaluate or recalibrate your results. Determine what went well, what can be improved, and how to execute it more effectively in the future. Discuss with friends, family, or coworkers your adjustments and ask for their perspective. Seeking counsel has saved many from making decisions that they would regret later. After you have completed this assessment, implement your adjustments, then rinse and repeat, as necessary.

Actor/Producer Will Smith said, "You only need a plan "A" because having a plan "B" distracts from plan "A." Put your energy and effort into the areas that will help you lead a fulfilled life. Living a purposeful life can bring us joy and extend the vitality of our lives. Focusing on additional or backup plans may cause complacency. How often have we completed introspective looks at our life and wondered, what have I accomplished over the last three or five years? What progress am I proud to share with others? If you can't answer these questions confidently, a change is needed. We have all heard the quote, "Doing the same thing expecting a different result is insanity." What do you plan to do about it? Shift your attitude, you got this!

REVIEW: SICK AND TIRED OF BEING SICK AND TIRED?

1. According to Reliable Plant, only ___ percent of people set goals for themselves. What's even more unfortunate is that out of the 20 percent of people who do set goals, only about ___ percent of people will succeed. Only a third of the people who set goals achieve them and of all people, which makes up ___ percent.
2. Discipline takes intentionality and much _____.
3. Set a date for one of your goals. Write out the roadmap to achieving that goal and inform your accountability partner.

_____
_____
_____

4. Set measurable goals with timelines and include an accountability partner. Goals must be _____, _____, and include dates that coincide with each milestone.
5. During the journey of achieving your goal, set a time to re-evaluate or recalibrate your results, this is called _____.

Key Notes From Chapter

- Motivation is an emotion, a general desire. Discipline does not rely on your emotions; it is a choice. You must decide that you are going to follow a routine to get your desired results.

- *Discipline picks you up when motivation drops you off.*

- Allow nothing to stop you from achieving your goals (yourself, people, issues, etc.) Life will always present you with challenges, but you control how you show up and manage them.

- Take the time to think of ways you can reward yourself after each milestone. Prioritize your wants and be proud of your accomplishments.

- Put your energy and effort into areas that will help you to lead a fulfilled life. Living a purposeful life can bring us joy and extend the vitality of our life.

PART V

Are You Really Sorry to Hear That?

"I'm sorry to hear that." "My condolences to you and your family." "My prayers and thoughts are with you" or sending the emoji of two hands coming together. "How old was she…oh, then she lived a long life." These are sadly classic statements we hear when we share news about someone's death. What if I told you that if you shared these types of statements with people who were hurting, you may have caused a disconnection between you and them. A wall was created as soon as you uttered one of those statements. We must learn and practice speaking out of empathy, not sympathy.

My grandmother, Wanda Ruth Johnson passed away at 84 in 2022. She was the last living grandparent I had from both sides of my family. People shared clichés that were supposed to bring some level of comfort but all it brought was aggravation and frustration. Grieving my Nanny was hard enough, and although people had best intentions, they made me feel worse. I found myself getting increasingly irritated as I shared the news of her passing as the days rolled by. Where has the human connection gone? Have we gotten so disconnected and cold toward each other that we now sound like robots? Although we hear news that tugs on our hearts, we no longer have the capacity to respond with sincerity and authenticity. What happened to compassion for each other? Then, I realized that many of us simply do not understand the difference between sympathy and empathy.

I've heard people say, "I feel empathy and sympathy for you," and I found it interesting. How can one extend both? It's like talking, as many would say, "from both sides of your mouth." Let's begin to understand the differences by defining each word. Bren Brown, an American Professor and Researcher, describes empathy as a skill that can bring people together and make people feel included, while sympathy creates an uneven power dynamic and can lead to more isolation and disconnection[22]. Statements like, "I'm sorry to hear that", My prayers for you…", "Sorry for your loss," etc., creates disconnection. We use them because we don't have the awareness and vocabulary to know we are operating out of self. The only way to truly connect with others is by understanding and relating with them in the moment, which is empathy. In contrast to sympathy which requires zero authentic connection. Both definitions discuss a power struggle of the words. Sympathetic words are received with a level of emptiness and disingenuity. We all can connect; however, we must be intentional about our posture to provide that space for others. Many times, we simply don't want to put in the effort, or we don't know how to be empathetic. Some of us use excuses such as "I don't want to be in people's business," "I don't know what to say," or "I don't want to say something that will make things worse." These are not justifications to fall into sympathy but an opportunity to show compassion. Following are some tools that will help you engage with others with sincerity.

EMPATHY STRATEGIES

1. *Awareness.* To connect with others, the work begins in the mind first. You must place yourself in another person's shoes. For example, if someone shares information with you about a friend who has passed away. Many of us might say "I'm sorry to hear that." Are you genuinely sorry to hear that news or have you used "I'm sorry" as a requirement before moving forward with the conversation? Placing yourself in someone's shoes requires you to place yourself in the same place in your memories. In that moment, you must think about someone who passed away in your life and identify the emotions that you felt. This requires work since most of us have learned to operate from autopilot and provide ready-made responses.

2. *Regulate.* After identifying the emotions that were coupled with the memory, you must speak from that place. Many times, we do not allow this process and we attempt to fix someone's problem by sharing how we handled our loss. For example, we may communicate the steps that we took to "get through" or encourage them to "be strong." Neither of these responses demonstrates empathy but sympathy. Empathy does not seek to fix the person or situation but seeks to understand and relate with them in the moment.

3. *Join their space.* When people are in an emotionally heightened state of mind, connecting with others can help alleviate some of the stress of their situation and allow for emotions to be processed. Remember, emotions cannot be destroyed, only transferred, or converted. Communication allows for that transfer and/or conver-

sion. As you decide to sit with them in their space, don't judge them or their situation. People need safety in these times and a judgmental statement can distract from your connection. Be open and allow the individual to open their heart. Often, no words need to be shared, but a hug or extending your arm around their shoulder communicates safety. When in doubt about how you can be there for another, simply ask them. They can share what they may need at the time.

HeartWork® Challenge

Following are statements that are commonly used in conversations, after someone has shared uncomfortable news. Place an "S" for the sympathetic statement and a "E" for an empathetic statement. Here's the situation, you are calling to check on a friend who you haven't heard from in a while. After speaking with her for a few moments, she shares that she has been feeling overwhelmed and depressed because her best friend of 20 years passed away. You provide the following statements[23].

1. "I'm sorry to hear that." _____

2. "I'm sorry for your loss." _____

3. "My prayers and condolences go out to you and their family." _____

4. "My thoughts and prayers are with you." _____

5. "Wow, that is tough to hear. I remember when my friend passed away, I was feeling overwhelmed and powerless. If you need to talk, I am here for you." _____

The correct answers are listed in the appendix.

Were you surprised to learn that many of those statements were based on sympathy? In many of the statements, you did not relate to your friend's situation. I know what many of you may be thinking since I hear this every time I facilitate a course. "Joanna, providing what happened to me would put the spotlight on me and not on my friend and isn't that selfish?" My response is always, "No, that is not selfish." When you communicate from your shared experiences, you are relating with your friend. You are not stealing the spotlight. If you communicate with sincerity from your heart, your friend will feel the emotion as you speak. Remember, emotions are an energy source. Those emotions that are stirred will act as a warm blanket and comfort your friend in the moment. At the end of the day, connection makes the difference in conversations not trying to fix the other person. Maya Angelou said, "I've learned that people will forget what you said, people will forget what you did, but people will never forget how you made them feel." How are you making people feel after they have spoken to you? Do your words build them up or do your words leave a toxic and cancerous trail? Only you can answer that question with honesty. I would encourage you to speak hope filled words to others. Be intentional in leaving conversations making the other person feel empowered after they have spoken with you.

Self-Empathy - HeartWork® Challenge

How empathetic are you in your words and behavior toward yourself? Are you extending empathy to yourself? Please rate yourself 1-5 and place the number under the statements below. One represents a level of weakness, five represents a level of strength. After you have rated yourself, add up your numbers, and place the total in the "TOTAL SCORE" area. I hope you accept the HeartWork® Challenge and gain insight into how empathetic you are to yourself.

1. I am intentional about filling my thoughts with positivity throughout the day.

    _____

2. I speak positive words to myself aloud throughout the day.

    _____

3. I am intentional about setting healthy boundaries for friends or family who are toxic.

    _____

4. I take time to sit alone and seek to understand what may have driven a passionate response.

    _____

5. I'm hard on myself because I know I can do better.

    _____

TOTAL SCORE: _____

Benefits of Self-Empathy

Self-empathy requires one to demonstrate a level of patience, grace, and mercy. These attributes are only obtained as you go through the challenge. It is easy for someone to say that they are a patient person, but how do they respond when their level of patience is tested? For example, you go to the grocery store at a time that is convenient for you and is normally a slow period for the store. As you walk into the store you look at the register and notice the line is almost halfway down the food aisle. Immediately you begin to feel irritated, frustrated, or powerless. What do you do? This is the time when your patience is tested. Do you walk back out of the store and decide you'll shop another day, or decide to complete your shopping and suffer through the wait?

Patience

Patience is defined as one's capacity to accept or tolerate delay, trouble, or suffering without getting angry or upset[24]. If you decided to walk out of the store, did you display patience in the moment? Your response to the situation will depict your level of patience and patience is the first step needed to be empathetic to yourself. Many times, when we fall short of our self-imposed expectations, we begin to judge and beat ourselves up. Then, we become critical of others as well. We judge them since we judge ourselves. We can't give out of a negative capacity, and we can't give what we don't have. For example, how can one give love when many of their interactions of love have been tainted by family and friends? As a result of tainted love, there is a lack of awareness of how to love oneself and others. A lack of awareness in these areas causes many broken people and broken relationships. Unfortunately, many of us have stayed in this cycle for years. *Unmet expectations (criticism) + negative thoughts = A repetitive pattern*. We must choose to do something different, and displaying patience to ourselves begins this process. But how do we embrace patience?

HeartWork® Challenge

Can you think of a time when you fell short of a goal? How did you treat yourself? Were you patient or did you throw the towel in on the situation? Write below.

_____
_____
_____

When you have fallen short of a self-imposed expectation, take the time to understand your emotions. Identify what you were feeling at that moment and why. Allow yourself to process any memories or emotions that may arise during this time. Don't abort the process! Begin to take note of these areas and trust the HeartWork®. Many times, we fall into traps and are unable to complete it because we don't give ourselves grace. What is grace?

Give Grace

Compassion International, an outreach ministry, defines grace as undeserved favor. Grace is not something that is earned but is freely given[25]. When you have not measured up to your expectation, extend grace. Grace doesn't cost you anything but allows hope and possibility to enter your mind. How does that look? You realize that you made an unhealthy decision. Take ownership of the decision and decide to discover your gains. What did you learn about yourself or others that will benefit you long term? What decisions would you make differently if you were in a similar situation? Are you willing to tell others about your experience, so they don't have to make the same mistake? Grace is something that keeps giving and giving and doesn't look for repayment. However, it must begin with extending grace to yourself. Unfortunately, many of us don't get to this place but life has a funny way of allowing us to repeat challenges until we adopt a new mindset. The reason many of us can't accept a new attitude is because we don't extend ourselves grace and mercy.

Be Merciful

What is mercy? Mercy is having compassion or forgiveness shown toward someone whom it is within one's power to punish or harm[26]. You are in the position to punish yourself with negative thoughts, speaking negative words, or deciding to completely give up on your goal. What decisions have you made in the past? Do you remember how you felt after you sentenced yourself? Did that strategy work or did it sustain your efforts? Did you ultimately get a good outcome? Probably not. So, what do you do? I'm glad you asked. When faced with scenarios in which you felt that you didn't give it your best effort, assess what you did, and discover the underlying reasons for the underachievement. Then decide that you will not extend the punishment that you may feel is warranted. Embrace mercy, pick yourself up, dust off any residue, and commit to trying again until your goal is accomplished.

Empathetic Strategies

What do a bad cop, bad doctor, bad lawyer, and bad teacher have in common? I know you may be thinking they are all bad. That is true, but the other commonality is that they are all human beings. When we begin to look at each other as human beings or look at people and think they could be our brother, sister, mother, etc., we will have a different approach to them. I passionately believe that when we choose to connect with ourselves and others with intent, it changes the nature of our relationships. We begin to see our hearts for each other. We become a society that shows care toward our friends, families, or neighbors. Thus, people will feel the connection and not feel empty, alone, or isolated. Here are some strategies you can keep with you along your journey of showing empathy.

1. *Awareness*. Be aware that your perspective and view of a situation is not the only or best perspective. I'm reminded of the saying, "There are always three sides to a story, your truth, their truth, and the actual truth." Before you lead with your perspective and judgment, think about what may be driving that perspective. Has your upbringing, culture, religion, etc., contributed to your response? Begin to think about how their upbringing, culture, religion, etc., may have played a role in their actions. If you are unsure of their experiences, seek to understand and ask questions.

2. *Regulate*. Slow down your thoughts and actions and take a deep breath. Intentionality allows you to engage the frontal lobe and make a decision that has not been emotionally hijacked. Think about how your words or behavior will impact you or the relationship 10 minutes later or after 24 hours. After considering these factors, would

you still make that decision? Give yourself the space and grace to make an emotionally intelligent decision.

3. *Discipline.* Incorporate these strategies daily and be committed to the process. Society has produced people who are robotic and disinterested in others. "I'm sorry to hear that" and prayer emoji hands signify this disconnect. We must choose to open our hearts, be vulnerable, and trust people again. It is time to let go of the weighty emotional baggage and live again. All of this is possible if we don't give up on ourselves and embrace this lifelong journey of HeartWork®.

TESTIMONY CORNER

A participant in an emotional intelligence class I facilitated gave me a call. When I answered he reminded me of some of the lessons he learned about self-awareness and empathy and how it impacted his life. He came to the realization that what he learned from his parents wasn't always the best advice. They had shared coping methods and strategies in dealing with relationships and children that were toxic. However, it was what they had the capacity to give. He recognized their capacity and decided to love and understand that they did the best that they could. He also discovered that he had some areas that needed improvement and began to do his HeartWork®. As a result of his intentionality, his relationship with his parents and wife got much better.

During the call, he shared further details about his wife. He included her in the principles he learned from the course. His wife was intrigued after seeing how the information was helping him. The more he shared EI with her, the more she began to recognize how she was showing up in life. She began to identify trauma in her life with her mother that needed healing. So, as a couple, they decided she would go through the same course he attended. They felt this was essential since each of them had unresolved childhood trauma and experiences that were subconsciously driving their decisions. They were a few months away from conceiving a baby and did not want to impose any toxic beliefs or values onto their child. I was blown away when I heard their reasoning for additional EI sessions. It's not often that people choose to learn EI to prevent generational patterns.

During the wife's training, roots of unforgiveness to her mom and feelings of unworthiness (because of abuse) were discovered. As we worked through these challenges, she felt the weight begin to leave her heart. After the training, she had to have a few conversations and had several letters to write. Gratefully, she embraced the challenges and has now moved on with her life without the weight of unforgiveness or unworthiness. Although they still have other challenges, they are determined to take the time to pause and seek to understand each other through their conflicts. They have decided that they will be intentional in raising their child without the toxic cycles they endured.

This testimony is a clear representation of empathy. Instead of the husband getting angry with his wife about how she interacted with him, he remembered how he dealt with his childhood traumas. He ultimately was patient with her and showed her mercy and grace throughout her healing. He also took it upon himself to encourage her to get the help she needed. Gladly, she accepted the help, and her soul is much better because of her intentionality. This world would be so different if we all took the time to slow down and seek to understand people before we judge them like this couple. What will you do?

REVIEW: ARE YOU REALLY SORRY TO HEAR THAT?

1. According to Daniel Goleman, _____ is the ability to understand and relate to the emotions of others or yourself.

2. I shared with you that my beloved grandmother passed away. Write an empathetic response using the strategies provided. Avoid "I'm sorry to hear that" and other cliché responses.

_____
_____
_____

3. Which area will you work on first in an effort to show empathy toward yourself?

_____
_____
_____

4. _____ doesn't cost you anything but allows hope and possibility to enter your mind.

5. Turn to _____ and begin to think about how one's upbringing, culture, religion, etc., may have played a role in their actions.

Key Notes From Chapter

- Connecting with others begins in the mind first. You must place yourself in another person's shoes and decide to revisit memories to speak from that emotion.

- Many of us have stayed in a negative cycle for years. However, *unmet expectations + negative thoughts = A repetitive pattern*. We must choose to do something different, and displaying patience to ourselves begins this process.

- Self-empathy requires demonstrating patience, grace, and mercy toward oneself. These attributes are only obtained as one goes through the challenge.

- Take a deeper look into yourself and others with intent, it will change the nature of our relationships and allow for heart connections.

- Let go of the weighty emotional baggage and live again. Don't give up on yourself and embrace this lifelong journey of HeartWork®. Your future self will thank you.

ACKNOWLEDGMENTS

When I first learned about emotional intelligence, my mind was blown. I wondered why these principles weren't mandatory teachings required in school. Why didn't every employee, leader, executive, or business owner know about EI? Why weren't we using these principles throughout life? These questions motivated my desire to become certified in emotional intelligence. As I began my journey, I had no idea how this information would challenge my understanding as a woman, wife, mother, friend, business owner, etc. I had to be the first recipient of this HeartWork® to understand, and this work changed my life forever! As I continue to do my HeartWork®, I am becoming a better woman, friend, business owner, etc. This is a process in which you will forever grow. I also knew that I couldn't keep this information to myself. I wanted as many people as possible to experience the freedom, peace, confidence, understanding of worth, etc. that I experienced. So, I decided to write this book. During the book writing experience, I never imagined how the content would freely flow. I'm so grateful to the Holy Spirit, which empowered and inspired me through this experience. I pray that you were inspired and empowered as you read this book.

I must thank several people who played a role in the success of this book. I want to thank my husband, Michael Avin, for supporting and pushing me throughout the years. You have been so supportive and patient with my acts of faith. I want to thank our kids,

Ryan Williams-Jenkins, Shawn Avin, Brianna Avin, and Gabriel Avin. You all have been instrumental in helping me work through challenges and supported me in more ways than you may know. My siblings, Sharod Jones, Ahkeem Darden, Wanda Darden, Leah Toussaint, Rudy Darden, and Faith Darden, thank you. We went through many of our struggles under the same roof; I am honored that even through adulthood, we continue to support each other. Thank you for helping to shape the woman that I am today.

Finally, I thank Joanna Darden and Leroy Darden, my parents. Unfortunately, my father passed away while I was young, and my mother continues the vision. My mom always challenges us to "Make a difference in your corner." Her words set the foundation of the work that I am committed to seeing to the end. Mom, I can't express my gratitude to you enough. You suffered a lot of persecution from family, friends, and others, but you never lost your faith in God. Your walk with God provided the blueprint for my relationship with Him. Thank you for the patience and consistency that you continually share with me.

Thank you to my close friends and extended family, who have supported me throughout this experience. Dr. Traci Lynn, you encouraged me to "make my frame bigger." My Pastor, Bishop Henry Fernandez, continues to challenge us to, "maximize our potential." Everyone I didn't mention, you know who you are, thank you. My heart has been overwhelmed by your willingness to see my endeavors succeed.

Thank you to everyone who supported me in the publishing of this book. My proofreader, editor, and publicist. You helped to launch the first of many to come.

This is just the beginning of my journey. Expect to see more books and pay me a visit as I tour a city near you. My next publication in this series will focus on the social aspects of emotional intelligence. Social Awareness, resolving conflict in a healthy manner, communicating effectively, understanding your biases and cultural differences, etc. will also be examined. Now that you understand how you are showing up to others, you can be proactive in the way that you influence and manage your external relationships.

Thank you for purchasing this book. Become a part of the HeartWork® Challenge and invite others to do their soul work. I hope ~~that~~ this book has blessed you as it blessed me in writing it.

APPENDIX

HeartWork® Challenge - Empathy or Sympathy

1. "I'm sorry to hear that." **Sympathy**

2. "I'm sorry for your loss." **Sympathy**

3. "My prayers and condolences go out to you and your family." **Sympathy**

4. "My thoughts and prayers are with you." **Sympathy**

5. "Wow, that is tough to hear. I remember when my friend passed away, I was feeling overwhelmed and powerless. If you need to talk, I am here for you." **Empathy**

Self-Empathy Score

5-10: You have your challenges in managing negative thoughts. Create affirmations that counteract the repetitive toxic thoughts. Make this a daily practice, and you will see change.

11-20: You are managing your thoughts; however, external drivers may occasionally take you off course. Be intentional about counteracting your thoughts with words of truth spoken aloud, and rinse and repeat as needed.

21-25: You are doing a great job of empowering yourself. Begin to empower others with the strategies that have worked for you.

CITATIONS

1. Weigard, Alexander. "Study Shows Men, Women Share Similar Emotional Highs and Lows: Psychiatry: Michigan Medicine." Psychiatry, 29 Oct. 2021, medicine.umich.edu/dept/psychiatry/news/archive/202110/study-shows-men-women-share-similar-emotional-highs-lows.
2. Posted May 17, 2019, by UWA. "Our Basic Emotions Infographic: List of Human Emotions." UWA Online, 20 May 2019, online.uwa.edu/infographics/basic-emotions/#:~:text=The%20Six%20Basic%20Emotions,%2C%20anger%2C%20surprise%20and%20disgust
3. Landry, Lauren. "Emotional Intelligence in Leadership: Why It's Important." Business Insights Blog, 3 Apr. 2019, online.hbs.edu/blog/post/emotional-intelligence-in-leadership#:~:text=Emotional%20intelligence%20is%20defined%20as,popularized%20by%20psychologist%20Daniel%20Goleman.
4. Dr. Travis Bradberry, Emotional Intelligence 2.0 (TalentSmart, 2009)
5. Timothy Jorgensen, Spirit Life Training, (Destiny Image, 2016)
6. Timothy Jorgensen, Spirit Life Training, (Destiny Image, 2016)
7. Levine, Micheal. "Logic and Emotion." Psychology Today, 2012, www.psychologytoday.com/us/blog/the-divided-mind/201207/logic-and-emotion
8. Dr. Travis Bradberry, Emotional Intelligence 2.0 (TalentSmart, 2009)
9. "The Limbic System." Queensland Brain Institute - University of Queensland, 15 May 2023, qbi.uq.edu.au/brain/brain-anatomy/limbic-system#:~:text=The%20limbic%20system%20is%20the,and%20fight%20or%20flight%20responses
10. "Understanding the Teen Brain" Understanding the Teen Brain - Health Encyclopedia - University of Rochester Medical Center, www.urmc.rochester.edu/encyclopedia/content.aspx?ContentTypeID=1&ContentID=3051#:~:text=Adults%20think%20with%20the%20prefrontal,awareness%20of%20long%2Dterm%20consequences
11. Admin. "Major Difference between Human and Animal Brain." BYJUS, 10 July 2020, byjus.com/biology/difference-between-human-brain-and-

animal-brain/#:~:text=Humans%20are%20considered%20to%20be,compared%20to%20the%20animal%20brain

12. Lee, Ye-Seul, et al. "Understanding Mind-Body Interaction from the Perspective of East Asian Medicine." Evidence-Based Complementary and Alternative Medicine: eCAM, 2017, www.ncbi.nlm.nih.gov/pmc/articles/PMC5585554/
13. Lee, Ye-Seul, et al. "Understanding Mind-Body Interaction from the Perspective of East Asian Medicine." Evidence-Based Complementary and Alternative Medicine: eCAM, 2017, www.ncbi.nlm.nih.gov/pmc/articles/PMC5585554/
14. "Heart Disease Facts." Centers for Disease Control and Prevention, 14 Oct. 2022, www.cdc.gov/heartdisease/facts.htm#:~:text=Heart%20disease%20is%20the%20leading,groups%20in%20the%20United%20States.&text=One%20person%20dies%20every%2034,United%20States%20from%20cardiovascular%20disease
15. Goleman, D., Boyatzis, R. & McKee, A. (2002). Primal Leadership: Realizing the Importance of Emotional Intelligence, Harvard Business School Press: Boston
16. Kauflin, Jeff. "Only 15% of People Are Self-Aware -- Here's How to Change." Forbes, 29 June 2021, www.forbes.com/sites/jeffkauflin/2017/05/10/only-15-of-people-are-self-aware-heres-how-to-change/?sh=1b10c4e82b8c
17. Content Team, Mind Tools. "Home." MindTools, www.mindtools.com/aunxs99/8-ways-to-improve-self-regulation. Accessed 17 May 2023
18. Verma, Prakhar. "Destroy Negativity from Your Mind with This Simple Exercise." Medium, 16 Apr. 2021, medium.com/the-mission/a-practical-hack-to-combat-negative-thoughts-in-2-minutes-or-less-cc3d1bddb3af
19. Languages, Oxford. "Definition Oxford Languages." Google Search, www.google.com/search?sxsrf=APwXEddyC75uYzCNoN7UbD0VqAnSB6AuSg%3A1684411946804&q=motivation&si=AMnBZoGI0zZC-9B5VLYtFM_IzEeH1MpKhCHBkZAunQyK6E4rReVebqo2SIzvXV2j7KTpAz8k_HbK3Ro3vGjfAasIMgTsLTn221zq-oEQoGSa236UvlpsSDg%3D&expnd=1&sa=X&ved=2ahUKEwjL_fm96_7-AhWGZjABHfi3DlQQ2v4IegQIHhA_&biw=1396&bih=685&dpr=1.38. Accessed 18 May 2023
20. "Discipline Definition & Meaning." Translated by Merriam-Webster, Merriam-Webster, 2023, www.merriam-webster.com/dictionary/discipline
21. Nina. "How Many People Reach Their Goals? Goal Statistics 2023." Goals Calling, 19 Feb. 2023, goalscalling.com/goal-statistics/

22. Twenty One Toys. "Dr Brené Brown: Empathy vs Sympathy." Twenty One Toys, twentyonetoys.com/blogs/teaching-empathy/brene-brown-empathy-vs-sympathy. Accessed 18 May 2023
23. 2011-2023, (c) Copyright skillsyouneed.com. "What Is Empathy?" Skills You Need, 2011, www.skillsyouneed.com/ips/empathy.html#:~:text=Daniel%20Goleman%2C%20author%20of%20the,others'%20emotional%20responses%20and%20reactions.
24. Barbian, Thomas. "The Skill of Patience." Columbia Metropolitan Magazine, 5 Mar. 2019, columbiametro.com/article/the-skill-of-patience/#:~:text=Patience%20is%20defined%20as%20%E2%80%9Cthe,become%20a%20more%20patient%20person
25. Compassion. "What the Bible Says about Grace." Bible Verses About Grace – Compassion International, 2023, www.compassion.com/christian-faith/bible-verses-about-grace.htm#:~:text=God's%20grace%20is%20usually%20defined,a%20part%20of%20God's%20character
26. The Oxford Pocket Dictionary of Current English.. Encyclopedia.Com. 5 May. 2023." Encyclopedia.Com, 18 May 2023, www.encyclopedia.com/philosophy-and-religion/bible/bible-general/mercy

www.ingramcontent.com/pod-product-compliance
Lightning Source LLC
LaVergne TN
LVHW070938070526
838199LV00035B/648